W9-BXA-201

GOOD EATING EVERY DAY

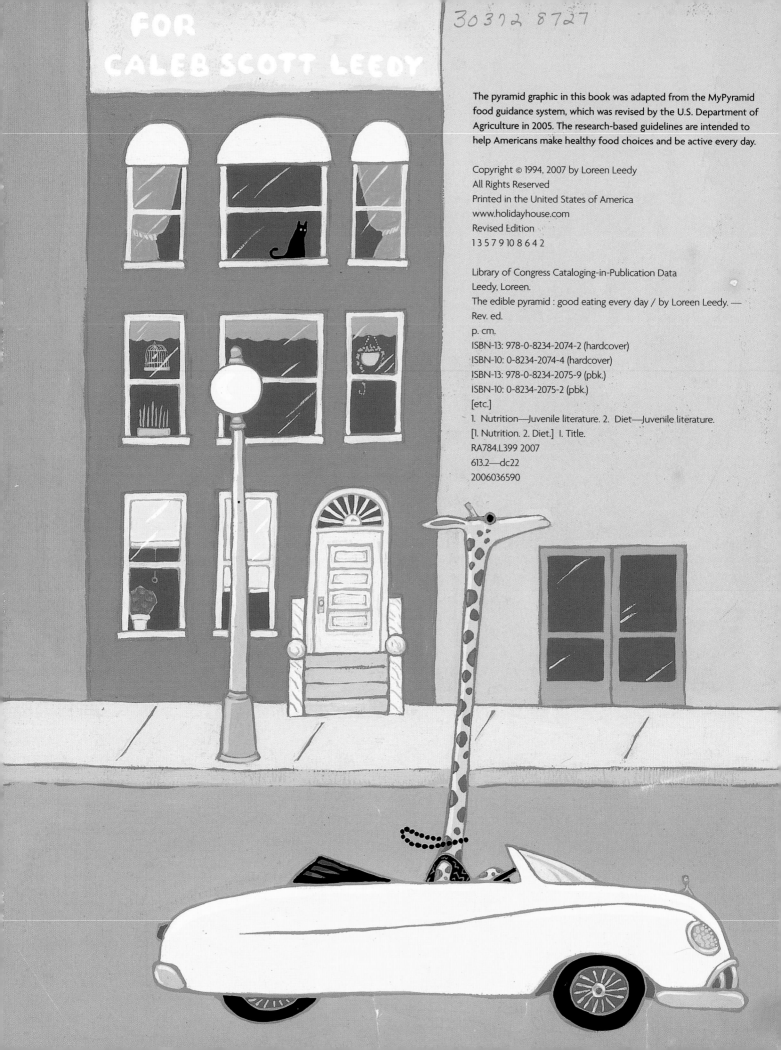

FOR
CALEB SCOTT LEEDY

The pyramid graphic in this book was adapted from the MyPyramid food guidance system, which was revised by the U.S. Department of Agriculture in 2005. The research-based guidelines are intended to help Americans make healthy food choices and be active every day.

Library of Congress Cataloging-in-Publication Data
Leedy, Loreen.
The edible pyramid : good eating every day / by Loreen Leedy. —
Rev. ed.
p. cm.
ISBN-13: 978-0-8234-2074-2 (hardcover)
ISBN-10: 0-8234-2074-4 (hardcover)
ISBN-13: 978-0-8234-2075-9 (pbk.)
ISBN-10: 0-8234-2075-2 (pbk.)
[etc.]
1. Nutrition—Juvenile literature. 2. Diet—Juvenile literature.
[1. Nutrition. 2. Diet.] I. Title.
RA784.L399 2007
613.2—dc22
2006036590

The Edible Pyramid

GOOD EATING

EVERY DAY

written & illustrated by

Loreen Leedy

Holiday House • New York

On the day of the grand opening of The Edible Pyramid restaurant, customers lined up to get inside.

GRAND OPENING
Welcome to our restaurant!
I hope their flies are fresh.

Our pyramid menu helps you plan good meals. Try to eat foods from each group every day.

Grains

Vegetables

6 ounces a day

2½ cups a day

GRAINS

Let's start on the left side of the pyramid. Here are the BREADS we serve. They are in the GRAINS group.

whole wheat

cornbread

We have PASTA in amazing shapes!

GRAINS

shell

ziti

A C F
alphabet
B K O

GRAINS can be prepared in many ways.

brown rice

bran muffin

millet

VEGETABLES

Now we move over a row in the pyramid. VEGETABLES come in delicious colors.

tomato

eggplant

peas

carrot

broccoli

corn on the cob

potato

onion

peach

cherry

banana

cantaloupe

apple

lemon

strawberry

Swiss cheese

cream cheese

Cheddar cheese

mozzarella cheese

MEAT and BEANS

We also serve MEAT, SEAFOOD, POULTRY, and EGGS.

beef

meatballs

ham

flounder

tuna

clams

shrimp

"POULTRY" means chicken, turkey, and other birds we eat.

chicken

chicken soup

turkey burger

turkey

boiled eggs

fried egg

The menu says to eat 6 ounces of GRAINS a day. How much is that?

Let's count ounces... 2 of bread and 1 of crackers equals 3 ounces just in this meal!

◄ 1 slice bread = 1 oz.

◄ 1 slice bread = 1 oz.

◄ several crackers = 1 oz.

The size of your serving depends on **your** size and activity level.

This is a serving for me.

This is a serving for me!

Sometimes foods are mixed together, such as in pizza. Just estimate how much of each food group is in your serving.

May I take your order?
fish
4 oz. MEAT
bun
2 oz. GRAINS
tomato
lettuce
1/2 cup
VEGETABLES
sauce
OILS
milk
1 cup MILK
I'll have a fish sandwich
and a glass of milk.

Kids should exercise for at least one hour every day. But let's finish eating first!

AUG   2007